Just For NOT!

Christmas Carols

MW00669398

Contents

The wonderful drawings on the cover and interior of this book were supplied by students who visited Cherry Lane Music Company for *Take Our Daughters To Work Day*. The day is sponsored by The MS Foundation For Women. Cherry Lane gratefully acknowledges these colorful and creative contributions from our young artitsts. We wish to thank all those involved in making the day and experience a wonderful success.

Arranged by Carol Klose

Copyright © 1997 Cherry Lane Music Company
International Copyright Secured All Rights Reserved

The music, text, and graphics in this publication are protected by copyright law. Any duplication or transmission, by any means, electronic, mechanical, photocopying, recording or otherwise, is an infringement of copyright.

For a comprehensive listing of Cherry Lane Music's songbooks, sheet music, instructional materials, videos and more, check out our entire catalog on the Internet. Our home page address is http://www.cherrylane.com

Angels We Have Heard On High

French-English

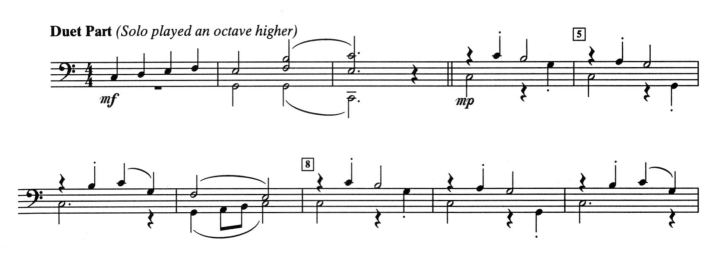

This Arrangement © 1997 Cherry Lane Music Company
International Copyright Secured All Rights Reserved

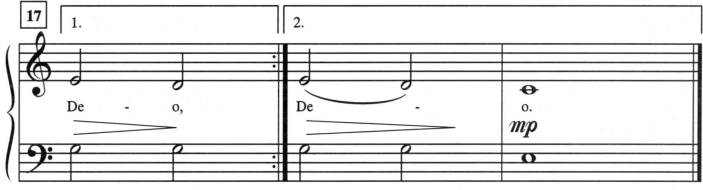

Deck The Halls

Old Welsh

Joyfully

Begin here for solo

Duet Part *(Solo played an octave higher)*

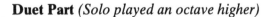
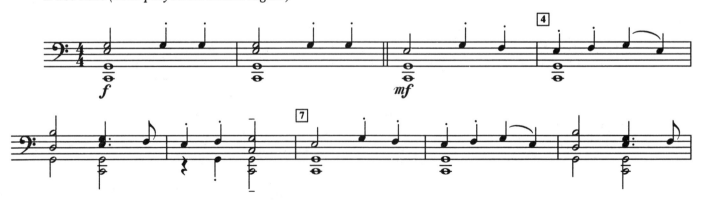

This Arrangement © 1997 Cherry Lane Music Company
International Copyright Secured All Rights Reserved

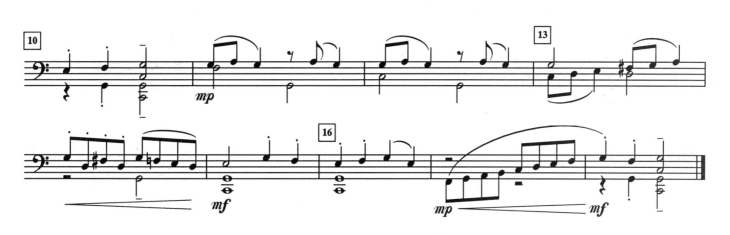

The First Noël

Traditional English

Moderately slow

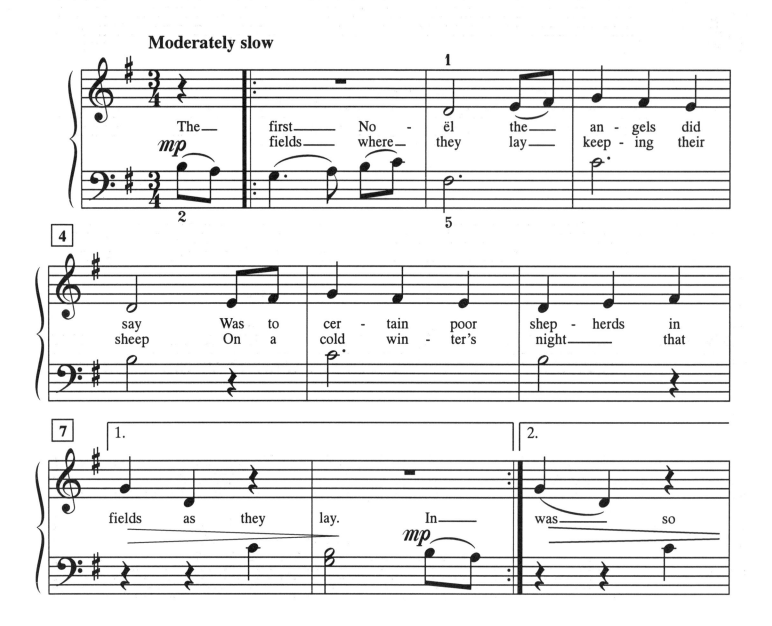

Duet Part *(Solo played an octave higher)*

This Arrangement © 1997 Cherry Lane Music Company
International Copyright Secured All Rights Reserved

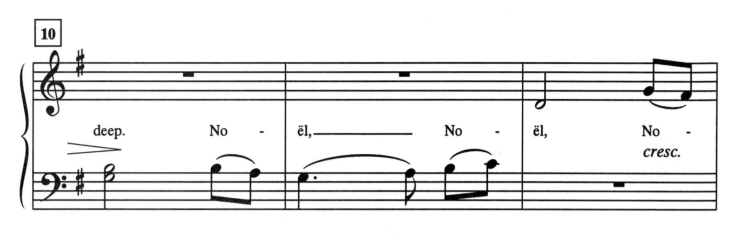

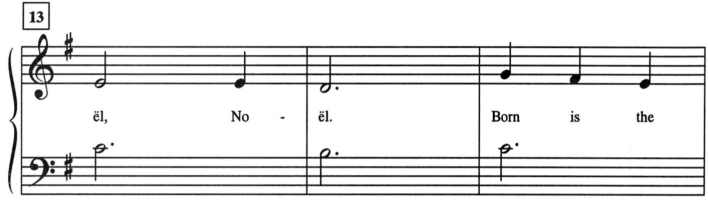

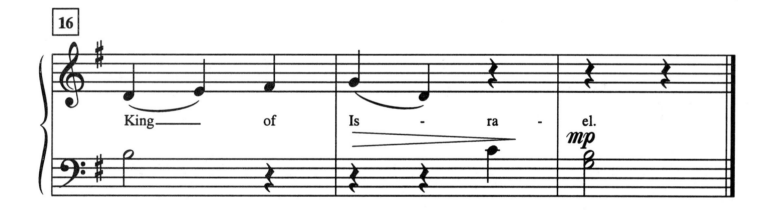

God Rest Ye Merry, Gentlemen

Traditional English

Duet Part

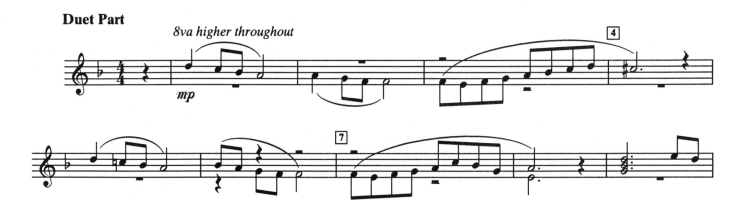

This Arrangement © 1997 Cherry Lane Music Company
International Copyright Secured All Rights Reserved

Sa - tan's pow'r when we were gone a - stray; O—

tid - ings of com - fort and joy, com - fort and

joy, O— tid - ings of com - fort and joy.—
rit.

rit. *p*

Hark! The Herald Angels Sing

Words by Charles Wesley
Music by Felix Mendelssohn-Bartholdy

Duet Part (Solo played an octave higher)

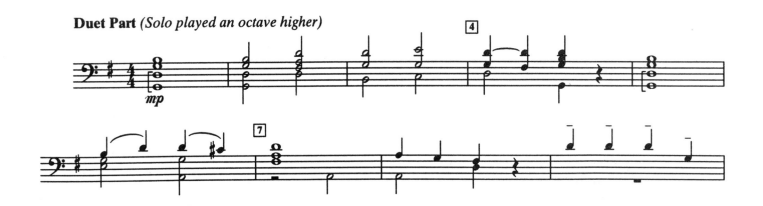

This Arrangement © 1997 Cherry Lane Music Company
International Copyright Secured All Rights Reserved

It Came Upon A Midnight Clear

Words by Edmund H. Sears
Music by Richard S. Willis

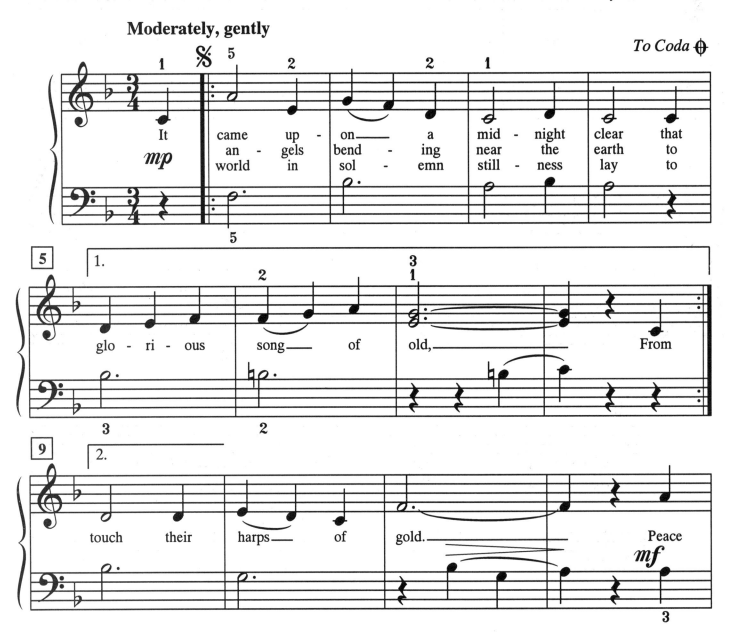

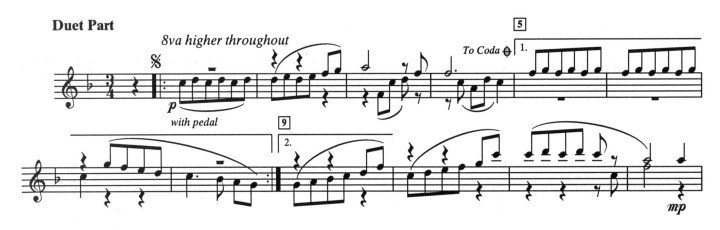

Duet Part

This Arrangement © 1997 Cherry Lane Music Company
International Copyright Secured All Rights Reserved

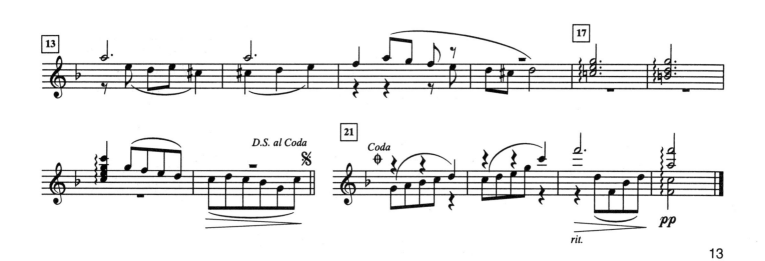

Jingle Bells

Words and Music by James Pierpont

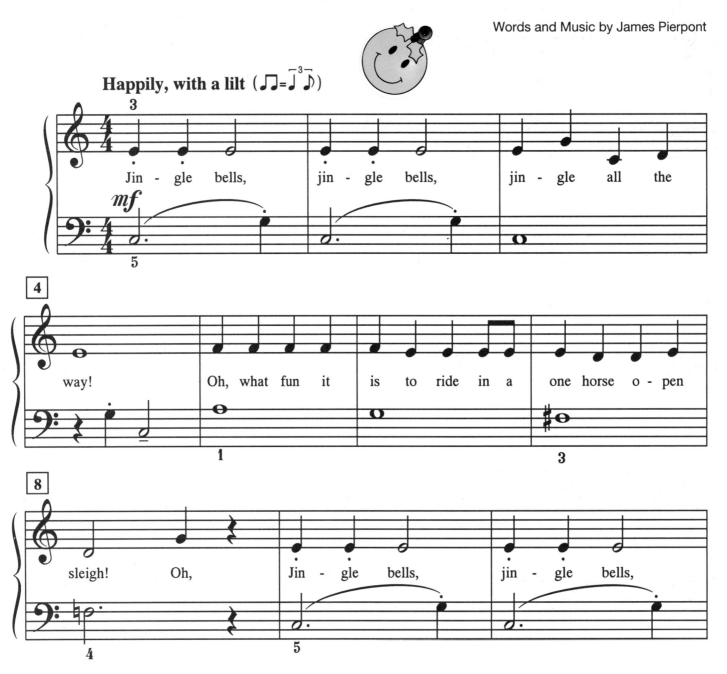

Happily, with a lilt

Duet Part (*Solo played an octave higher*)

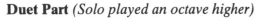

14

This Arrangement © 1997 Cherry Lane Music Company
International Copyright Secured All Rights Reserved

jin - gle all the way! Oh, what fun it

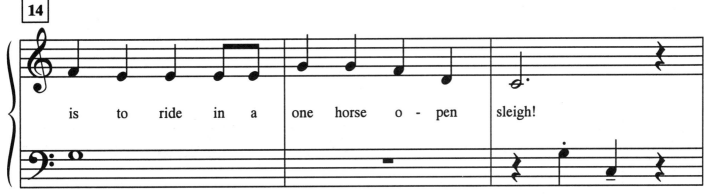

is to ride in a one horse o - pen sleigh!

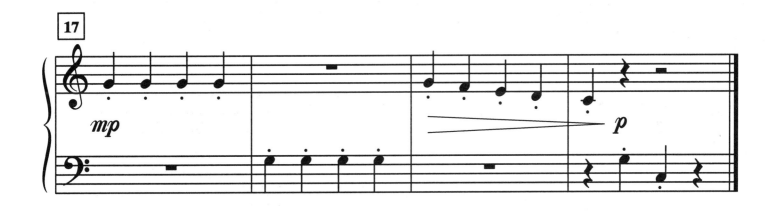

mp

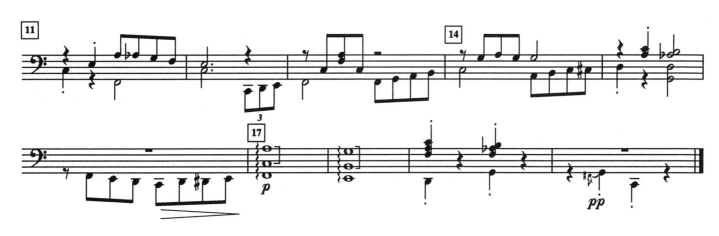

Joy To The World

Words by Rev. Issac Watts
Music by Lowell Mason

With spirit

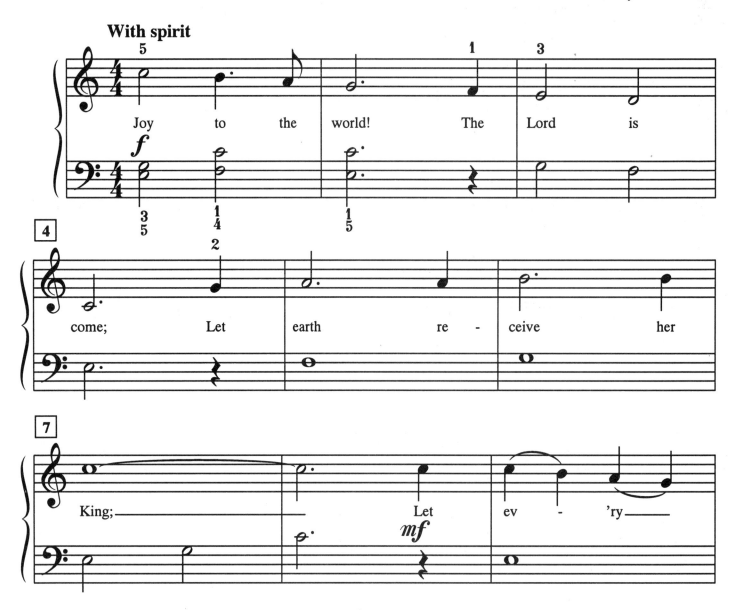

Joy to the world! The Lord is come; Let earth re - ceive her King;_____ Let ev - 'ry_____

Duet Part *(Solo played an octave higher)*

This Arrangement © 1997 Cherry Lane Music Company
International Copyright Secured All Rights Reserved

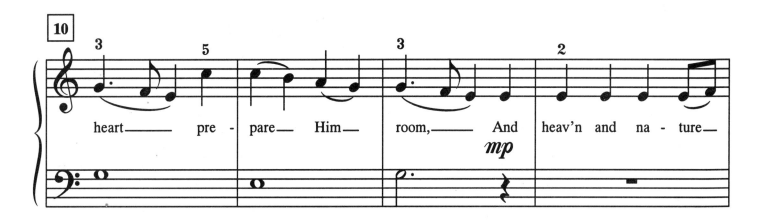

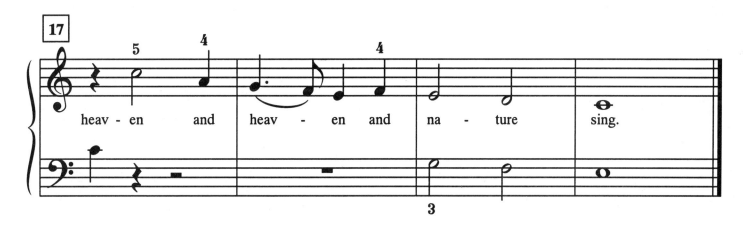

O Come All Ye Faithful

Words and Music by John Francis Wade

Triumphantly, not too fast

Duet Part (*Solo played an octave higher*)

This Arrangement © 1997 Cherry Lane Music Company
International Copyright Secured All Rights Reserved

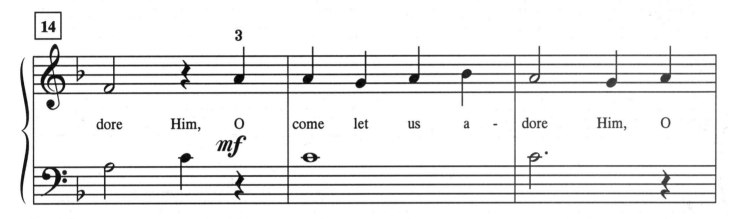

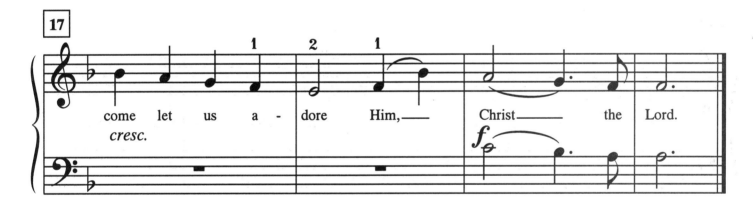

O Little Town Of Bethlehem

Words by Phillips Brooks
Music by Lewis H. Redner

Duet Part *(Solo played an octave higher)*

This Arrangement © 1997 Cherry Lane Music Company
International Copyright Secured All Rights Reserved

by. Yet in thy dark streets shin - eth the

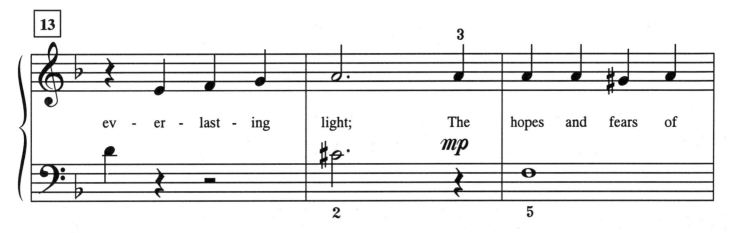

ev - er - last - ing light; The hopes and fears of

all the years are met in thee to - night.

Silent Night

Words by Joseph Mohr
Music by Franz Gruber

Tenderly

Si - lent night! Ho - ly night!

All is calm, all is bright.

Round yon vir - gin moth - er and Child!

Duet Part *(Solo played an octave higher)*

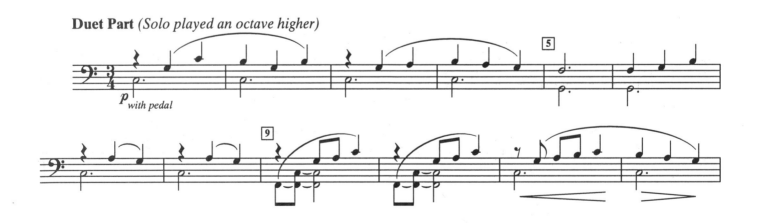

This Arrangement © 1997 Cherry Lane Music Company
International Copyright Secured All Rights Reserved

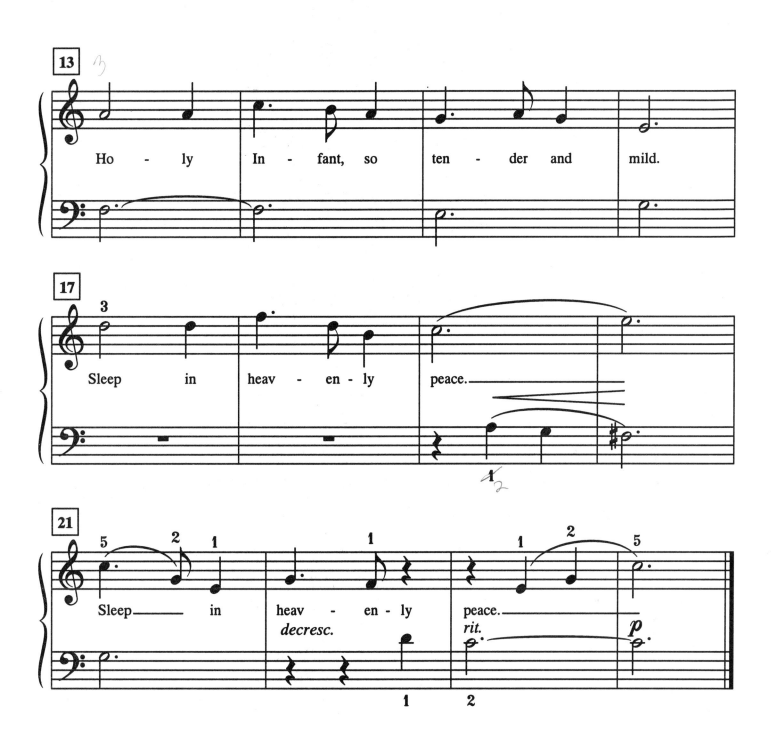

We Three Kings

Words and Music by John Henry Hopkins, Jr.

Mysteriously

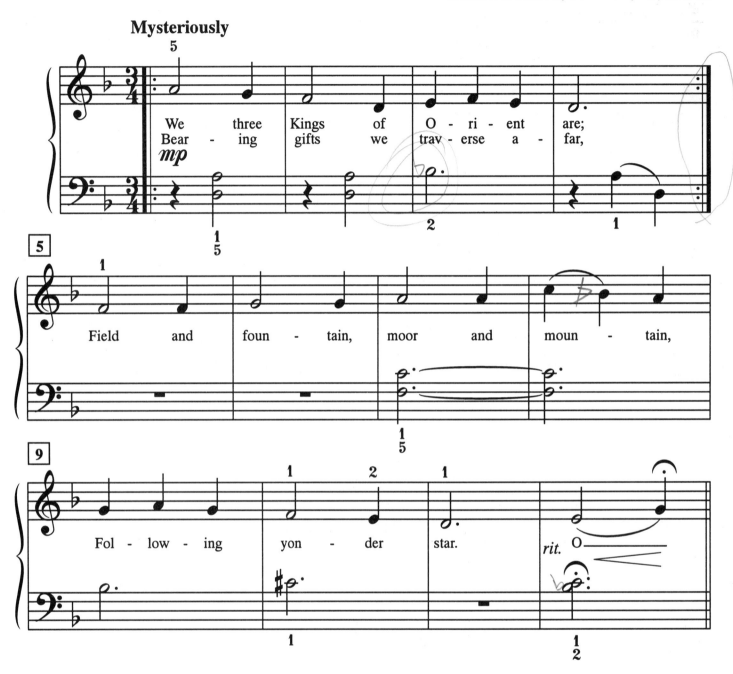

We three Kings of O - ri - ent are;
Bear - ing gifts we trav - erse a - far,

Field and foun - tain, moor and moun - tain,

Fol - low - ing yon - der star.

Duet Part *(Solo played an octave higher)*

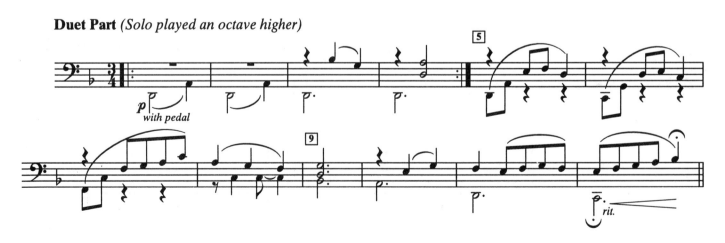

This Arrangement © 1997 Cherry Lane Music Company
International Copyright Secured All Rights Reserved

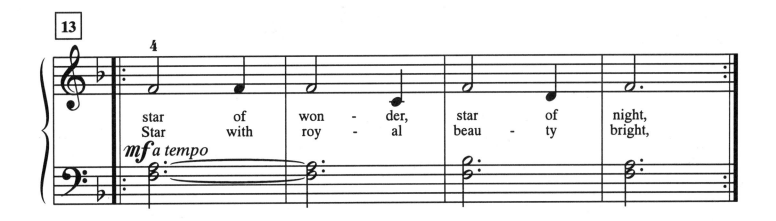

star   of   won - der,   star   of   night,
Star   with   roy - al   beau - ty   bright,

mf a tempo

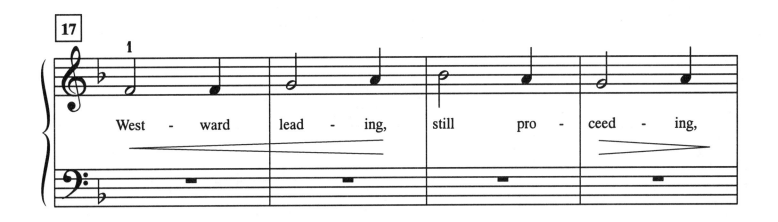

West - ward   lead - ing,   still   pro - ceed - ing,

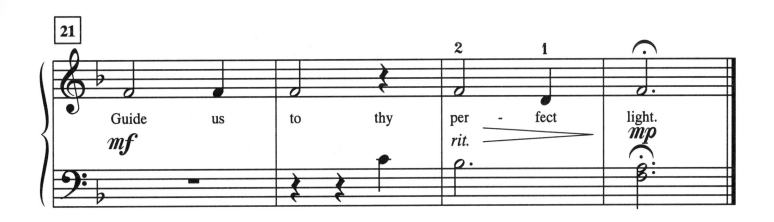

Guide   us   to   thy   per - fect   light.

mf   *rit.*   *mp*

mp
a tempo

cresc.

mp

rit.   *p*

We Wish You A Merry Christmas

English Folk Song

Lively Waltz tempo

Begin here for solo

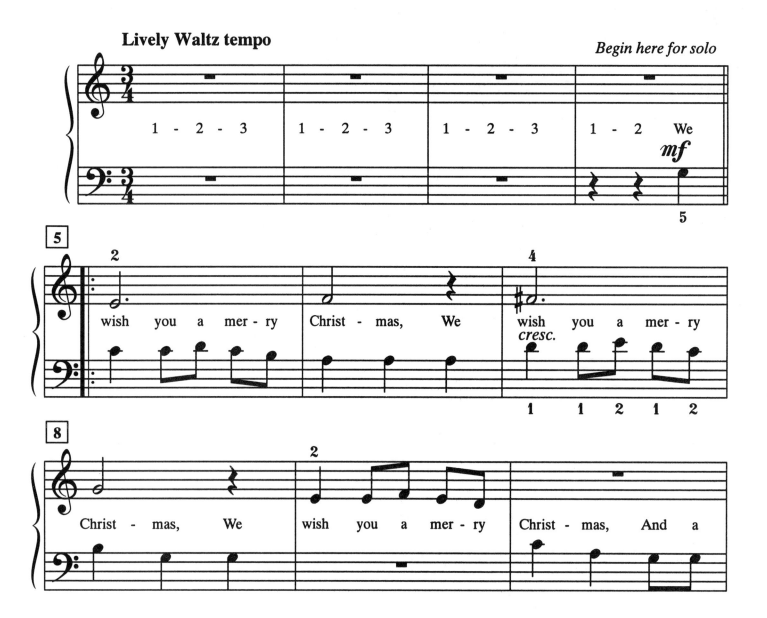

Duet Part *(Solo played an octave higher)*

This Arrangement © 1997 Cherry Lane Music Company
International Copyright Secured All Rights Reserved

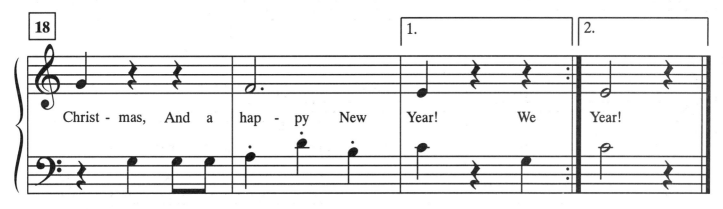

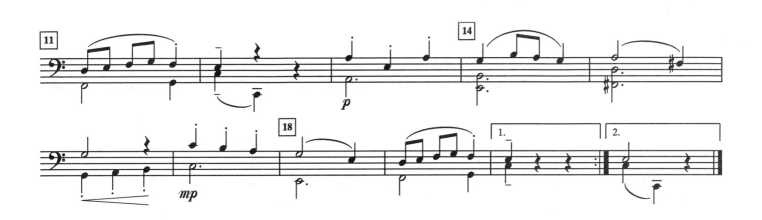

What Child Is This?

Words by William Chatterton Dix
16th-century English tune "Greensleeves"

Moderately, with expression

This Arrangement © 1997 Cherry Lane Music Company
International Copyright Secured All Rights Reserved

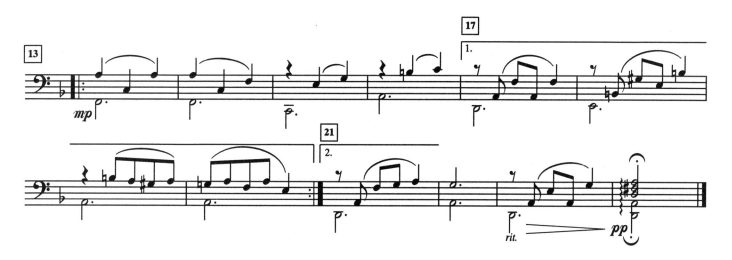

Notes
on the music
Commentary by Carol Klose

Angels We Have Heard On High

Although the exact origin of this carol was unclear for many years, it is now generally thought to have originated in France in the 1700s. The words were translated in England in 1862, and the carol was first published in America in 1916 in the form we know it today.

Performance Tips: This arrangement should be played at a moderately fast tempo. The left-hand part is easy since there are only three bass-clef notes in the accompaniment: middle C, and G and E below. When the melody moves to the left hand (measures 7, 8, 11, 12, 15, and 16), it should sound as smooth and *legato* as if played by one hand.

Deck The Halls

Sometimes known as "Deck The Halls With Boughs Of Ivy," the music for this lively seasonal tune originated in 16th-century Wales. As early as 1784 it was given its English lyrics by an anonymous writer, but it was not until 1881 that it was first published.

Performance Tips: "Deck The Halls" should be performed at a fast, lively tempo, felt in "two" (beats 1 and 2 in the first group, and beats 3 and 4 in the second, with a slight accent on beats 1 and 3). However, practice should begin slowly, with close attention paid to the staccatos and slurs, fingering, and dynamics. The notes with *tenuto* marks (–) on beat 3 (measures 6, 10, 14, and 18) should be accented slightly and held for two full beats.

The First Noël

When this song originated as a folk carol in 16th-century England, the proper spelling would have been "The First Nowell" ("Noël" being a French word). In 1833, the traditional words and music were published in a collection of carols as the standard Christmas song familiar to us today.

Performance Tips: Observing the dynamics and playing with a smooth *legato* touch will help bring out the rise and fall of this simple but beautiful melody. When played without the duet, the verse (from the beginning through the second beat in measure 10) may be played one octave higher than written. The chorus (measure 10, beat 3, to the end) can continue one octave higher, or can be played *loco* (as written).

God Rest Ye Merry, Gentlemen

This carol is one of the many that have come down to us from 16th-century England. The first publication of the traditional words and music to the song appeared in 1827. In his 1843 work *A Christmas Carol*, Charles Dickens mentions "God Rest Ye Merry, Gentlemen" as being sung by a caroler chased away by Scrooge on the streets of London.

Performance Tips: Although written in a minor key, the mood of this carol is bright and cheerful. The duet part for "God Rest Ye Merry, Gentlemen" is made up of its own secondary melody (called a "countermelody" or *obbligato* part) which is played *above* the solo part and harmonizes with the solo melody. In this song, the duet performer will sit to the *right* at the piano. The duet part should always be played slightly softer than the solo.

Hark! The Herald Angels Sing

The majestic quality of "Hark! The Herald Angels Sing" is the result of the musical genius of Felix Mendelssohn, who composed the music in 1840 for two male choirs and brass instruments, using the words written by Charles Wesley nearly one hundred years earlier. The choral composition celebrated the 400th anniversary of Gutenberg's invention of the printing press.

Performance Tips: The song should be played in a strict march-like tempo, with a slight accent on notes with *tenuto* marks (–) in measures 9 and 11. After measure 9, the melodic phrases are traded between the right and left hands. The solo performer can separate these phrases by releasing the last note just before the bar line in measures 10, 12, 14, 16, and 18.

It Came Upon A Midnight Clear

Two men from Massachusetts are responsible for this American carol. In 1849, Edmund H. Sears wrote the words, and in 1850 Richard S. Willis composed the music. However, neither was written with the other in mind. The words and music were soon after combined by an unknown person and published in a book of hymns.

Performance Tips: This song takes many surprising turns in both the left- and right-hand parts, so it should be practiced carefully hands alone, especially for fingering and accidentals. The duet part provides a gentle background *above* the solo, with the duet performer sitting to the *right*.

Jingle Bells

"Jingle Bells," the first great American popular Christmas song, was composed in 1857 by James S. Pierpont, a Boston native. It is said that he wrote it for a Sunday school class, but the song soon became a favorite throughout the land.

Performance Tips: This arrangement should be played at a moderately bright tempo, with crisp staccatos where indicated. The left-hand G's on beat 4 (measures 1, 2, 9, and 10) should be played and released with a light touch, just enough to provide a rhythmic pulse after beat 3. The coda, in measures 17 through 20, provides a delightful tag ending to the song.

When played with the duet part, this arrangement takes on a jazzy twist, with pairs of eighth notes played as triplets (♫ = $\overline{J\,\,J}^{3}$).

Joy To The World

The words to "Joy To The World" were written by the Englishman Isaac Watts in 1719. The music, sometimes attributed to George Frederick Handel, was actually written by Lowell Mason, a well-known American composer of hymn tunes. The carol was first published by Mason in the 1830s.

Performance Tips: In this arrangement, the fingering for the right-hand part should be followed closely, since all eight notes of the C major scale are played in the right-hand melody. Although the song begins *forte* (loud), the left-hand accompaniment should be slightly softer throughout, so the sweeping melody can be heard above all.

O Come All Ye Faithful

The original version of this carol, known as "Adeste Fideles," was written in Latin in the 1740s by the English Catholic music teacher John Francis Wade. It was later translated into English by Frederich Oakeley in 1852, but is still sung in both languages.

Performance Tips: The melody notes in the solo part of this arrangement are divided between both hands. The performer should play with a connected, *legato* touch, trading the melody notes smoothly from hand to hand. The sudden *mezzo piano* (moderately soft) dynamic at the end of measure 12 begins a *crescendo* to the *forte* (loud) marking in the last two measures. Observing these dynamics will create a dramatic and triumphant ending to the song.

O Little Town Of Bethlehem

The words for this song date from 1868, when a clergyman from Philadelphia, Phillips Brooks, wrote some verses describing a trip he had taken to the Holy Land. Later he asked his friend Lewis H. Redner to compose a melody to go with the poem for a Sunday school program. The result was "O Little Town Of Bethlehem," which was first published in 1920 as a popular Christmas carol.

Performance Tips: The arrangement should be played with expression and feeling, with a smooth *legato* touch, especially when the melody notes move between the hands. The left-hand part, which is mostly in the F major five-finger position, should be practiced alone at first for fingering and accidentals.

Silent Night

An interesting turn of fate was responsible for the creation of this famous carol. On Christmas Eve in 1818, in the town of Oberndorf, Austria, the church organ had broken down. As a result, the priest and church organist composed a new song "Stille Nacht, Heilige Nacht," to be accompanied by guitar at Mass that night. Father Joseph Mohr wrote the German words, and Franz Gruber composed the music. An organ repairman later obtained a copy of the music and began the spread of this simple but beautiful song around the world. In 1881 the German version was translated into English as "Silent Night."

Performance Tips: This arrangement should be played softly, keeping the left-hand accompaniment especially quiet. When played without the duet part, the solo performer can use the damper pedal, changing the pedal every two measures from the beginning through measure 16. From measure 17 through 22 the pedal should be omitted, then a single pedal added for the last two measures.

We Three Kings

This unique carol dates back to 1857. Both the words and the music were composed by the American John Henry Hopkins, who wrote the song as a Christmas gift for some relatives.

Performance Tips: There are two sections in this song. The first part (measures 1 through 12) begins in a minor key (D minor), giving the melody a haunting quality. The second part (measures 13 through 24) begins cheerfully with major key harmonies (F major), but ends softly in the original melancholy minor key. The dynamic markings and ritards in this song provide the performer with a musical map that will help convey the mood of these two sections. Fingering should be carefully observed, since both hands move between the D minor and F major five-finger positions.

We Wish You A Merry Christmas

Few songs convey the happiness and good will of the Christmas season as well as "We Wish You A Merry Christmas." The origins of this musical Christmas card are set in the West Country of England, probably in the 1500s.

Performance Tips: The melody notes in the solo arrangement are played mainly by the left hand. The right-hand harmony notes (in measures 5, 6, 7, 8, 11, 19, 20, and 21) should be played softly above the melody. The left-hand part is made easier because the notes lie mostly within the G major five-finger position. The only exception is in measure 7, where finger 2 crosses over the thumb, then back. For variety, the solo part can be played staccato through beat 1 in measure 12.

What Child Is This?

Although it is one of today's most beloved Christmas carols, "What Child Is This?" is in fact based on a song known as "Greensleeves," composed anonymously in England in the 1500s. "Greensleeves" was so famous that it was mentioned around 1596 by Shakespeare in his play "The Merry Wives Of Windsor." In 1865 the Englishman William Chatterton Dix borrowed the melody and wrote the lyrics for the Christmas carol version.

Performance Tips: The solo part should be practiced slowly, hands alone at first, to observe fingering and accidentals. When played as a solo, the first half of this arrangement (measures 1 through 12) can be played an octave higher, with the second half played either an octave higher or *loco* (as written).